DEVELOPMENT OF EFFECTIVE TEAM

:

A HANDBOOK

Hiriyappa.B, Ph.D.

DEDICATION

To the readers who love reading my books

Contents

Preface
Team Intention
Managing Functions of Team
Team Effectiveness
Kinds of Groups
Team Dynamics
Group Development
Types of Groups
Turning Groups into Effective Teams

Preface

Group Dynamics and Team Building is immensely helpful to those who are willing to work with a team and wish to attain team leadership and work as a project lead of an organization.

1

Team Intention

INTRODUCTION

In this chapter, you will get to know what it is like to develop a team and to know the team, importance of a team, team intention and scope, features of successful teams, basic team rules, team meeting responsibilities, What makes a good team, team functions, team management, team effectiveness, understanding group behavior in an organization, what a group is, features of a group, characteristics of a mature group, types of work groups, team dynamics, importance of group dynamics, group norms, group cohesiveness, factors influencing group cohesive-ness, group development/stages of a group's formation, types of groups, advantages of group decisions, disadvantages of group decisions, effectiveness and efficiency of group decision making, techniques for improving group decision making, turning groups into effective teams and developing and managing effective teams.

DEFINITION OF TEAM

A team member must know how a team is defined according to The Wisdom of Teams published by Harvard Business School Press in 1993.

"A team is a small number of people with complementary skills who are committed to a common purpose, performance goals and approach for which they hold themselves mutually accountable". It reveals the following things as outlined:

A team comprises any group of people or animals linked to a common purpose. A group in itself does not necessarily constitute a team.

A team is a small group of people with complementary skills committed to a common purpose and set of specific performance goals.

It consists of two or more individuals who co-ordinate activities to accomplish a common task or goal.

Simply said, it is a group of people with a goal.

It refers to a group of people who work well together.

IMPORTANCE OF TEAM

You can understand the importance of a team as outlined:

Build commitment, purpose and partnership of your team by reviewing issues critical to their development.

Develop guidelines for team productivity by addressing norms for decision-making and limitations of authority.

Create a collective vision of what your team can become in the next year.

Build an action plan to move them towards sustained team effectiveness.

Team members must "get on the same page" regarding areas critical to performance.

Teams must revisit their missions and their role to ensure continued high performance; Teams play an important role in the operation of strategic management process in organizations. They facilitate in streamlining the process and increasing its efficiency and effectiveness. Building an effective management team entails consideration of several critical things in an organization.

A team and its work can be influenced by the predominant emotions of its members and teams can improve their emotional intelligence by understanding the tendencies of the group as a whole and learning to manage them effectively.

New teams can avoid the usual confusion of a "team start-up," enabling them to solidify more quickly into a focused and unified work group.

DEFINING TEAM INTENTION AND SCOPE

An effective team leader is bound to define team intention and the scope towards work as follows.

He selects team members and specifies to each team member their functions and duties in the team.

It clearly defines roles and responsibilities of all members in the team.

It helps to identify external customer needs, expectations and requirements and in this way, helps to achieve customer satisfaction.

It identifies internal customer needs, expectations and requirements and in this way, achieves employee satisfaction in the team.

It involves complete preliminary feasibility study of pro-jects and its impact and benefits towards an organization.

It helps in identifying costs, timing and constraints in the team and its project.

It identifies documentation process and methods that will be involved during the time of project process in an organization.

It develops a program plan (if project is a go) or other intended plans for the start and will help to complete a predefined schedule in an organization.

FEATURES OF SUCCESSFUL TEAMS

If you want to make successful teams, you must be bound to follow these things.

Successful teams are involved in proper management, directed and focused to a particular task in the team.

Every successful team has to build their own identity to get a project, plan the project, start the project and finish the project and management of the projects in an organization.

A team's performance and efforts are based on e-account-ability and measurements in terms of quality, quantity and price in an organization.

Teams have corporate champions for the achievement of a project and getting new projects which can happen only with the influence of the previous project's performance.

Teams should have to fit into the organization's rules, regulation and work culture.

Teams should be ready to handle cross-functional duties and responsibilities towards the projects and for the accomplishment of project tasks and goals within the stipulated time.

Teams should have proper planning in policy formula-tion, implementation and control of the project.

Teams should estimate the cost and benefit analysis of each project and measurement of performance in terms of monetary benefits and non-monetary benefits for team members in a team.

Proper guidance, suggestion and recommendation should come from team members about projects that are related to the details and completion of the project with cent percent quality.

Proper interaction among the team members is essential in a team.

Coordination and cooperation is needed among the members in the team and the organization or client.

BASIC TEAM RULES

Every member in a team must be aware of the basic rules in a team.
Basic team rules are listed below:

Determine if there should be a meeting in an organization.
Decide who should attend the meeting and work, and deciding on important authorizations (?) job in an
organization.

Provide advance notices to team members and project managers in an organization.

Maintain meeting minutes or records in an organization, its detail and its approval from team members.

Establish ground rules for essential requirements for the project which is relating to the job.
Provide and follow an agenda in a meeting.

Evaluate meeting results and focus on main objectives and tasks in an organization.

TEAM MEETING RESPONSIBILITIES

If you want to become an efficient team member, you should know about team meeting responsibilities. Team meeting responsibilities are as outlined:

Clarify goals and objectives of the meeting.

Have all team members participate in an organization. Listen to every member's views and opinions in the meeting.
Summarize all issues in the meeting.
Stay on track on the meeting's tasks and objectives. Manage time in the meeting.

Test for consensus between all team members in an organization.

Evaluate the meeting process in a systematic manner and finds reasons for the results.

Establish proper communication among the team and its members.

A team person should consult the group first, and then make the final decision.

The team or group should make the decision based upon majority rule or consensus.

WHAT IS A GOOD TEAM?

After this section, you will be able to evaluate yourself on knowing how to develop a good team. A good team is one which follows the following issues for welfare of the project and an organization:

Commitment to common objectives: goals, mission and vision of an organization.

Defined roles and responsibilities: clearly specified nature of work, project and terms and conditions that are in relation with the job.

Effective decision systems, communication and work procedures: these are very important to lead the team with success.

Good personal relationship among the team members and the client in an organization.

Good teams define the problem before jumping to solutions. Good teams have some type of structure with defined roles.
Good teams encourage new ideas and allow issue related conflict and solution of the conflict

The first step is to get to know each other, team members and client details and project details for carefully planning the formulation of a policy, implementation of the policy and control project tasks for accomplishment of goals and objectives in an organization.\

2

Managing Functions of Team

INTRODUCTION

With this chapter, you will learn how to manage functions in a team efficiently and effectively to accomplish vision and mission of a project.

A team is a group of people working towards a common goal. Team building is a process of enabling them to achieve that goal. A team involves the intelligent scanning of the environment, awareness of the functioning of the team, flexibility or readiness to change, tolerance of ambiguity and difference within the team, a preparedness to accept uncertainty as changes occur.

Facilitation

A team is either small or big. It plays a significant role in per-forming tasks by applying each member's special intellectual, professional and business skills.

Team leaders are in a tough spot. Most are managers who have been given new roles as their departments have evolved into functional and cross-functional teams. Unfortunately, the skills that helped them to be successful as managers don't necessarily apply in an organization.

Through practice and feedback, team leaders must learn the skills they need to effectively maximize a team's energy, thinking and resources. This helps empower teams as they meet to move forward on issues, solve problems and make decisions.

The purpose of assembling a team is to accomplish bigger goals than any that would be possible for the individual working alone. The aim and purpose of a team is to perform, get results and achieve victory in the workplace and marketplace. The very best managers are those who can gather a group of individuals together and mould them into a team. Here are ten key differentials to help you mould your people into a pro-active and productive team.

Understandings the nature of work. In a group, members think they are grouped together for administrative purposes only. Individuals sometimes cross purpose with others. In a team, members recognise their independence and understand both personal and team goals are best accomplished with mutual support. Time is not wasted struggling over "turf" or attempting personal gain at the expense of others.

Ownership/Leadership. In a group, many members tend to focus on themselves because they are not sufficiently involved in planning the unit's objectives. They approach their job simply as a hired hand. "Castle Building" is com-mon. In a team, members feel a sense of ownership for their jobs and unit, because they are committed to values based common goals that they helped in establishing.

Creativity and Contribution. In a group, members are told what to do rather than being asked what the best approach would be. Suggestions and creativity are not encouraged. In a team, members contribute to the organization's success by applying their unique talents, knowledge and creativity to team objectives.

Trust among the team members. In a group, members distrust the motives of colleagues because they do not understand the role of other members. Expressions of opinions or disagreement are considered divisive or non-supportive. In a team, members work in a climate of trust and are encouraged to openly express ideas, opinions, disagreements and feelings. Questions are welcomed.

Common and committed to work understandings. In a group, members are so cautious about what they say that real understanding is not possible. Game playing may occur and communication traps be set to catch the unwary. In a team, members practice opens and honest communication. They make an effort to understand each other's point of view.

Focused on personal development. In a group, members receive good training but are limited in applying it to the job by the manager or other group members. In a team, members are encouraged to continually develop skills and apply what they learn on the job. They perceive they have the support of the team.

Learning conflict resolution. In a group, members find themselves in conflict situations they do not know how to resolve. Their supervisor/leader may put off intervention until serious damage is done, i.e. a crisis situation. In a team, members realise conflict is a normal aspect of human interaction but they view such situations as an opportunity for new ideas and creativity. They work to resolve conflicts quickly and constructively.

Encouraging participative decision making. In a group, members may or may not participate in decisions affecting the team. Conformity often appears to be more important than positive results. Win/lose situations are common. In a team, members participate in decisions affecting the team but understand that their leader must make a final ruling whenever the team cannot decide, or when an emergency exists. Positive win/win results are the goals at all times.

Defined clear leadership. In a group, members tend to work in an unstructured environment with undetermined standards of performance. Leaders do not walk the talk and tend to lead from behind a desk. In a team, members work in a structured environment, they know what boundaries exist and who has final authority. The leader sets agreed high standards of performance and he/she is respected via active, willing participation.

Active and passionate commitment. In a group, members are uncommitted towards excellence and personal pride. Performance levels tend to be mediocre. Staff turnover is high because talented individuals quickly recognise that otherwise it is a problem for the group. In a team, this isn't the case.

TEAM MANAGEMENT

After learning about team management, you will able to administrate, manage, and buildup a highly resourceful team. The common definition of team management is as follows.

Team management is the direction of a group of individuals that work as a unit in an organization. Effective teams are result-oriented and are committed to project objectives, goals and strategies in an organization.

3

Team Effectiveness

INTRODUCTION

A team leader knows how to develop a team to be effective in completing a project. Team effectiveness is based on the performance of the team and its members in task and objectives in an organization:

Teams are proliferating in business organization because of their ability to achieve quality results quickly and effectively.

A team is ready to push to get the job done, and to pro-vide excellence in work in a client organization.
It achieves the goals of an organization.

It provides an opportunity to share leadership qualities among the team members in a team.

It is involved in effective decision-making process in an organization.

Building team effectiveness engages team members in a focused discussion about their work as a team and how the team achieves success.

It helps in gaining clarity and commitment regarding the team's purpose, partnership and productivity which yields a better team relationship.

PERFORMANCE NEEDS

Your ability to know how to develop performance and needs of a team is very important in determining the team effectiveness in an organization. These are some ways to do so, as follows:

Building commitment towards the team's purpose and partnership by reviewing issues critical to their development in an organization.

Developing guidelines for team productivity by addressing norms for decision-making and limitations of authority in team.

Creating a collective vision of what your team can become in the next year.
Building an action plan to move them toward sustained team effectiveness.

APPLICATION

In this section, you will get to know how to develop team application in a team. Team application is very important and significant towards team effectiveness in an organization:

Team members must get on the application i.e. relating to the project regarding areas critical to performance.

Teams must revisit their missions and their roles to ensure continued high performance in an organization.

With proper team application, new teams can avoid the usual confusion of a "team start-up," enabling them to solidify more quickly into a focused and unified work group.

FACILITATION

Knowing how to make facilitation in a team will make you a smart team leader. Facilitation is one of the major keys in team effectiveness and is significant for the team and its effectiveness in an organization are as follows:

Team leaders are in a tough spot. Most are managers who have been given new roles as their departments have evolved into functional and cross-functional teams. A team and its members are facilities to achieve the planned performance in an organization.
Through practice and feedback, team leaders must learn the skills they need to effectively maximize a team's energy, thinking and resources. This helps in empower-ing teams as they meet to move forward on issues, solve problems and make decisions.

Work groups are playing a significant and very important role within today's business world. Work can be restructured around all types of groups and groups are needed in all kinds of organizations. Managers should understand the needs of the groups and its behavior concept in an organization in order to appreciate what groups can and cannot do within organizations and how groups function within and outside of an organization.

Any one member in a group can influence the behavior of the individuals in the group and teamwork in an organization. We will examine some basic characteristics of groups including the types of work groups, the development of informal groups, and the manner in which groups operate in the business world.

4

Kinds of Groups

INTRODUCTION

A team leader must understand group behavior in an organization to perform duties, roles and responsibilities and to accomplish committed tasks in a team. Groups have exhibited different behaviors in an organization. In this section, we're going to look at various aspects of group behavior, such group concepts, types of groups, stages of group developments and group dynamics.

What is a group?

A group is defined as two or more interacting and inter-dependent individuals who come together to achieve particular objectives in an organization.

It can also be defined as two or more freely interacting individuals who share a common identity and purpose. Groups have interdependence, interaction, and a common goal in an organization.

Groups differ from organizations due to the fact that organizations involve systematic efforts and are engaged in the production of goods and services.

Teamwork occurs when groups are able to work efficiently and effectively together to achieve organizational goals.

CHARACTERISTICS OF A MATURE GROUP

A team member should know the major characteristics of a mature group as outlined:

Team members are aware of each other's assets and liabilities.
In a team, individual differences are accepted.

The group's authority and interpersonal relationships are recognized in a team.

Group decisions are made through rational discussion in an organization.

Conflict is over group issues, not emotional issues in a team.

Members are aware of the group's processes and their own roles in an organization and its project.

TYPES OF WORK GROUPS

This section will make you aware of the types of work groups and how it works in an organization.
There are two types of work groups as outlined.

A formal group is a group officially planned and created by an organization for a specific purpose.

A command or functional group is a formal group consisting of a manager and all the subordinates who report to that manager.

Formal Group
Formal groups include command and task groups.

Each identifiable work group consisting of a manager and subordinates is a command group.

A linking is an individual who provides means of coordination between command groups at two different levels by fulfilling a supervisory role in the lower-level group and a subordinate role in the higher-level group.

Informal groups are natural social formations that appear in the work environment.

Informal Group

With the following description, you can know about an informal group's development and its commitment to serve in a project. An informal group is a group that is established by employees, rather than by the organization, in order to serve the group members' interests or social needs. Informal groups are unplanned groups.

An interest group is an informal group created to facilitate employees' pursuits of common concern.

Informal groups include interest and friendship groups.

A friendship group is an informal group that evolves primarily to meet employees' social needs.

5

Team Dynamics

INTRODUCTION

When you are working in a team, knowing how to develop team dynamics and its impact towards team spirit and performance is essential and this section will help you in understanding this concept.

Team dynamics are the unseen forces that operate in a team between different groups of people.

For example, in a small team of six people, there may be two people who have a particularly strong friendship.

IMPORTANCE OF GROUP DYNAMICS

You must know the significance of a team and the importance of group dynamics as outlined:

Formal and informal work groups are becoming increasingly important competitive factors in organizations due to changes in organizations.

Teamwork is the result of groups working together to effectively and efficiently achieves organizational tasks, vision and mission.

Formal groups include command and task groups in an organization.

Informal groups include interest and friendship groups.

Group dynamics is a useful way to analyze groups as systems that use input and engage in various processes or transformations, and produce outcomes in an organization.

Managers should be ready to help and bring about higher performance from formal work groups by weighing the characteristics of members who are assigned to particular groups.

Group members should have task-relevant expertise and appropriate interpersonal skills for accomplishment of tasks.

Group dynamics is a degree of diversity among group members that usually adds to performance in relation to the project.

Group training, particularly for diverse groups, have been found to be useful and helpful to other members in a team.

Team members may be attracted to a group for a number of reasons such as liking other members of the group, liking the activities, the goals or purposes of the group, or when the group satisfies an individual's need for affiliation, and when the group helps an individual achieve a goal outside the group.
In the case of absence of attraction, it can prevent the group from achieving high performance in an organization.

Team member roles in groups include group task roles, group maintenance roles, and self-performance.

The size of the group also plays a significant role in improving the group's performance.

In the case of mid-sized groups, it consists of five to seven members and this seem to be the optimum size in an organization.

Smaller groups can often intensify individual differences in team work.

Providing free riding is particularly likely when members exhibit individualism rather than collectivism.

In the case of a team, a manager can combat social loafing by several methods and assign few extra people to do the work. It is one key method to achieve tasks in a team.

Team dynamics can be improved by using other methods for measuring team performance like making each individual's work visible, providing individual feed-back, working with respect towards team members, measuring standards to actually understand what the group performance is, and giving suitable rewards to individual members in the team for enhancing group performance.

TEAM SYNERGY

Teamwork performance is dependent on the performance of team members in an organization. Sometimes, team performance is low due to negligence of the team and its members and sometimes performance is high when the work is planned, organized and controlled by team and its members. This process is called synergy.

Positive synergy is the force that results when the combined gains from group interaction (as opposed to individuals operating alone) are greater than group process losses.
Negative synergy is the force that results when group process losses are greater than any gains achieved from combining the forces of group members.

There are three key characteristics of a group that determine the synergy levels. These are listed below:

Group norms.
Group cohesiveness.
Group development.

GROUP NORMS

If you are working in a multinational culture team, you know of group norms. It refers to the standards (degrees of acceptability and unacceptability) for conduct that help individuals judge what is good or bad in a given social setting.

Group norms are culturally derived and vary from one culture to another.

Group norms are usually unwritten, yet have a strong influence on individual behavior.

Group norms may go above and beyond formal rules and written policies.

Norms are the behaviors of group members that are acceptable to the group.

Norms stem from explicit statements by supervisors and coworkers, critical events in a group's history, primacy and carryover behaviors.

Work groups norms are related to the performance, appearance, social measurement and allocation of resources.

Performance norms

It refers to the degree of hard effort that has to be put by all the team members in a team, how the work can be done and what the team output contribution is towards an organization.

Appearance norms

It refers to the instructions regarding appropriate dress code which is to be followed by a team and its members in an organization. It is based on the type of work that is done by the executives and different rank of employees in an organization.

Social arrangement norms

It refers to informal work groups and it is concerned with regulating social interaction in the group.

Allocation of resources norms

It refers to resource allocation in an organization in terms of pay, assignment of difficult jobs and allocation of new tools and equipment utilized by a team in an organization.

Reasons for groups to enforce norms

It helps to facilitate the survival of the group. It is to simplify or clarify role expectations.

It is to help group members avoid embarrassing situations.

It is to express key group values and enhance the group's unique identity.

GROUP COHESIVENESS

In this section, you will come to know about group cohesiveness and how to work in a multi-cultural environment.

Group cohesiveness refers to consequences of group communication, satisfaction, performance, hostility and aggression toward other groups, and a group's willing-ness to innovate and change.

Major factors influence the amount of cohesiveness in a group such as shared attitudes and values within the members of the group, and the amount and severity of external threats to the group.

It shares the group experiences in terms of recognizable successes, the degree of difficulty encountered in joining the group, and the size of the group.

FACTORS INFLUENCING GROUP COHESIVENESS

The development of group cohesiveness in a project purely depends on the group size, degree of dependency, physical distances, time spent together, severity of initiation, cooperation and threat history of past successes. These are the major factors influencing the group's cohesiveness in an organization.

The factors mentioned above will be explained in detail in the following pages.

Group size

A Small group size has a greater probability of being cohesive than larger groups in an organization.

When team size increases, in this circumstance, the possibility of agreement towards the common goal and mutual interaction decreases.

When team size increases, it restricts intergroup and intragroup communication and encourages the formation of sub-groups.

Degree of dependency

It is an aspect between degree of cohesiveness and dependency in an organization.

It requires greater attractiveness towards goals in an organization.

Greater the degree of dependency, greater the attraction and consequently higher the group's cohesiveness in an organization.

Physical distance

People working together at a very close distance are likely to have greater opportunity for interaction in an organization, and it is very important.

It enhances the free exchange of ideas, sharing problems and prospects in an organization.

Therefore, it develops closeness among the team members which leads to greater cohesiveness.

Time spent together

Time spent together and cohesiveness are positively related to people who meet frequently and spend time together for developing mutual attraction and interpersonal interaction.

During this time, team members develop friendship and communication among members in an organization.

Severity of Initiation

It is positively correlated to cohesiveness.
When strict admission procedures are prescribed for entry into a group, it is called severity of initiation.

In this case, the group becomes unique and elite in the eyes of other teams in an organization.

It arises out of natural human tendency which is shared among the team members and thus, they get benefits for their efforts in an organization.

Cooperation

It is the team spirit that is developed by all team members in a team.

It helps to share their personal opinion, suggestion and recommendation relating to group tasks, reward system in a team and teamwork.

Well-designed organizational structure promotes greater cooperation and in this way cohesiveness is enhanced.

Status

Status and cohesiveness are positively related in an organization.
Status is the identity of a team and its members and their tasks in an organization,

Status will come with dedication, achievement, growth and development of an organization.

Threat

It is also considered the determining factor of cohesiveness. External threat is unpredictable and uncontrollable.
Internal threat can be predictable and controllable.

It has an impact on the group, its identity and process in an organization.

United and strong teams can easily face threat in an organization.

History of Past Successes
It is a very important factor influencing the group's cohesiveness in an organization.

Past result, performance, growth and development are the stepping-stones towards future goals, mission and vision of an organization.

Teams will be evaluated based on the past results and analyzed, which helps in the interpretation of the future result for survival, growth and development of an organization.

6

Group Development

INTRODUCTION

When you have your own organization and work with a few projects, you are bound to learn about developing a group and it becomes an intellectual asset for an organization and thus will be able to operate and maintain very good interaction skills among the members and clients.

there are five stages that are involved in the development of groups: forming, storming, norming, performing and adjourning.

STAGE 1: FORMING

In this stage, you form a team and it involves the following activities as listed below:

Forming occurs when group members attempt to assess the ground rules that will apply to a task and to group interaction.

First stage is forming which determines the definition of the team, determines individual roles, develops trust and communication and forming defined the task its problem and strategy that identifies the information that is needed for forming of the team.
It defines the team leader's role including encouragement and maintaining open communication that helps the team to develop and follow team norms, which in turn help the team to focus on the task and deal with conflict constructively.
It defines the team role like keeping a record of team meetings, maintaining a record of team assignments and maintaining a record of the team's work.

It involves contacting resourceful people outside of the team and corresponding with the team's mentor and working to maintain good communication among team members and the client.

It defines the team norms and it raises questions like, how do we support each other? What do we do when we have problems? What are my responsibilities to the team?

STAGE 2: STORMING

You would like to know how to develop the concept of storming. Storming occurs when group members experience conflict with one another and they locate and attempt to resolve differences of opinion. Storming is the second stage in the formation of a team. During the storming stage, team members are involved in the following activities:
Team members realize that the task is more difficult than they imagined,

Team members have fluctuations in attitude about chances of success,

They may be resistant to the task and,
They may have poor collaboration.

Storming diagnosis is raising the following activities for formation of the team:

Do we have common goals and objectives?
Do we agree on roles and responsibilities?

Do our task, communication and decision systems work? Do we have adequate interpersonal skills?
It involves the negotiating conflict in the following sense:

It separate issues from problems and people in an organization.
It can be soft on people, hard on problems.

It looks for underlying needs and goals of each party rather than specific work in an organization.

It addresses the problem in the following issues in an organization:

It states team members' views in clear non-judgmental language.
It clarifies the core issues in an organization.

It focuses to listen carefully to each person's point of view.

It checks the understanding by restating the core issues in an organization.

STAGE 3: NORMING

In this stage, you'll know how to develop norming in a group. Norming occurs as group members begin to build the group's cohesion, as well as develop a consensus about norms for performing a task and relating to one another. During this stage, members accept the following factors:
their team,
team rules and procedures,

their roles in the team and,
The individuality of fellow members.

Team members realize their roles and behavior in an organization.

Team members develop competitive relationships which become more cooperative.

There is a willingness to confront issues and solve problems.

Teams develop the ability to express criticism constructively. There is a sense of team spirit in an organization.

STAGE 4: PERFORMING

Performing occurs when energy is channeled towards a task as norms support teamwork. During this stage, team members have the following qualities to perform their job at an organization:

Gaining insight into personal and team processes in an organization.

A better understanding of each other's strengths and weaknesses in a team and its members.

Having gained the ability to prevent or work through group conflict and resolve differences among the team members in the team in an organization.

Developing a close attachment towards the team.

STAGE 5: ADJOURNING

Adjourning occurs when group members prepare for disengagement as the group nears successful completion of its goals.
It involves the following issues as listed below:

Recipe for successful team commitment that shared goals and objectives.

Clearly define roles and responsibilities towards the team, the members and the teamwork.
Use the best skills of each member in the team.

Allows every member to participate and develop new ideas and solutions for problems in all areas.

Provide effective systems and processes in an organization.

Clear communication among the members in an
organization.

Beneficial team behaviors like well-defined decision procedures and ground rules.
Balanced participation in team decisions.
Awareness of the group process in an organization.
Good personal relationships among the team members in an organization.

7

Types of Groups

INTRODUCTION

In the section of the book, you will learn how to develop different types of groups and their application in different circumstances to complete the project within a stipulated time.

There are different types groups as outlined

INFORMAL GROUPS

It refers to a collection of people seeking friendship and acceptance that satisfies esteem needs.

It refers to members who belong to various divisions or sections irrespective of their jobs.

These groups are formed for solving any serious problems in an organization.

FORMAL GROUPS

It refers to a collection of people created to do some-thing productive that contributes to the success of the larger organization.
It can form line authority in a team.
These teams are formed for a specific purpose in an organization.

REFERENCE GROUPS

It refers to members who act as a reference for individuals and form groups on the basis of the reference individual from outside of an organization and frame personality by reference members of a team.

These groups directly or indirectly affect the individual's attitude who is either a member or not a member in an organization.

SMALL GROUPS

It consists of two to five people.

It is highly effective for decision-making process in an organization.
Team members are limited.

Communication is very fast among the team members in an organization.

This type of groups will take very speedy decisions in an organization.

FRIENDSHIP GROUP

It is formed by friends in an organization.
These groups are formed only to meet the needs such as belongingness and security in an organization.

TASK GROUPS

Task groups only concentrate on tasks of an organization.
These types of groups are ready to make decisions for
achievement of major tasks in an organization.

SELF MANAGED TEAMS

These teams define their own goals and tasks and for this purpose, form these types of groups outside of an organization.

SELF DIRECTED TEAM

These team members are working together in an organization and they are self-directed towards a common goal that will define discipline, compensation and achievement of an organization.

ADVANTAGES OF GROUP DECISIONS

Group decisions have certain advantages over individual decisions.

Provide more and complete information.
Generates more alternatives.

Increases acceptance of a solution. Increases legitimacy.

DISADVANTAGES OF GROUP DECISIONS

Time consuming.
Minority domination.
Pressures to conform, which can lead to group thinking.
Ambiguous responsibility.

EFFECTIVENESS AND EFFICIENCY OF GROUP DECISION MAKING

It depends on the following criteria which are used in defining effectiveness:
Group decisions tend to be more accurate.

Individual decisions are quicker in terms of speed. Group decisions tend to have more acceptances.

The effectiveness of group decisions tends to be influenced by the size of the group.
Groups should not be too large.

Groups also are not as efficient as individual decision makers.

TECHNIQUES FOR IMPROVING GROUP DECISION MAKING

Brainstorming is an idea-generating process that encourages alternatives while withholding criticism.

Nominal group technique is a group decision-making technique in which group members are physically pre-sent but operate independently.

8

Turning Groups into Effective Teams

INTRODUCTION

In this chapter, you will learn how to turn groups into effective teams in an organization. Work teams are formal groups made up of interdependent individuals, responsible for attaining goals. Most of us are probably familiar with the concept of a team. However, we may not be as familiar with work teams. All work teams are groups, but only formal groups can be work teams.

There are different types of teams. Four characteristics can be used to distinguish the different types of teams.

Teams can vary in their purpose or goal.

The duration of a team tends to be either permanent or temporary.

Team membership can be either functional or cross-functional.

Finally, teams can either be supervised or self-managed. Given these four characteristics, some of the most popular types of teams used today include the following:

A functional team is a type of work team that is composed of a manager and his or her subordinates from a particular functional area.
A self-directed or self-managed team is one that operates without a manager and is responsible for a complete work
process or segment that delivers a product or service to an external or internal customer.
A virtual team is one that uses computer technology to link physically dispersed members in order to achieve a common goal.
Finally, a cross-functional team is one in which individuals who are experts in various specialties (or functions) work together on various organizational tasks.

DEVELOPING AND MANAGING EFFECTIVE TEAMS

Teams aren't automatically going to magically perform at high levels. We need to look more closely at how managers can develop and manage effective teams.

There are eight characteristics associated with effective teams. These are as follows:

Clear goals.
Relevant kills.
Mutual trust.
Unified commitment.
Good communication.
Negotiating skills.
Appropriate leadership.
Internal and external support.

WHAT'S INVOLVED WITH MANAGING TEAMS?

When planning, it's important that teams have clear goals and that these goals be clear to and accepted by every member of the team.

Organizing tasks associated with managing a team include clarification of authority and structural issues.

Leading issues include such things as determining what role the leader will play, how conflict will be handled, and what the best communication process is.

Two important controlling issues include how to evaluate the team's performance and how to reward the team members.

One popular approach to group incentive plans is gain-sharing, which is a program that shares the gains of the efforts of group members with those group members.

In conclusion, a TEAM is a temporary or ongoing task group whose members are charged with working together to identify problems, form a consensus about what should be done, and implement necessary actions in relation to a particular task or organizational area.

TEAMS DIFFER FROM TASK FORCES IN TWO WAYS

Teams identify problems rather than merely reacting to problems identified by others.

Teams decide on a course of action and implement it, rather than leaving the implementation to others.

Teams are widely used today and are often, but not always, task groups from across command groups.

An entrepreneurial team is a group of individuals with diverse expertise and backgrounds who are brought together to develop and implement innovative ideas aimed at creating new products or services or significantly improve existing ones.

Self-managed teams, or autonomous work groups, are work groups given responsibility for a task area without day-to-day supervision and with authority to influence and control both the group membership and behavior.

Assessment of the situation is critical and in that, self-managing teams are not successful in all situations.

Group makeup and proper allocation of needed resources is important.
Team training and guidance in cultivating appropriate norms are important.

Managers need to remove performance obstacles and provide assistance to help the group continue to learn.

About the Author
Dr. Hiriyappa.B holds a PhD and works as an Assistant Professor in Government First Grade College, Karnataka, India.

www.ingramcontent.com/pod-product-compliance
Lightning Source LLC
Chambersburg PA
CBHW030507220526
45464CB00006B/2690